Sound Advice on

Recording &

Mixing Vocals

by Bill Gibson

447 Georgia Street
Vallejo, CA 94590
(707) 554-1935

Publisher: Mike Lawson
Art Director: Stephen Ramirez; Editor: Patrick Runkle
Cover image recording artist Kitaro's hand, Ocean Way Studios.
Photo courtesy Mr. Bonzai.

ProAudio Press is an imprint of artistpro.com, LLC
447 Georgia Street
Vallejo, CA 94590
(707) 554-1935

Also from ProMusic Press
Music Copyright for the New Millennium
The Mellotron Book
Electronic Music Pioneers

Also from EMBooks
The Independent Working Musician
Making the Ultimate Demo, 2nd Ed.
Remix: The Electronic Music Explosion
Making Music with Your Computer, 2nd Ed.
Anatomy of a Home Studio
The EM Guide to the Roland VS-880

Also from MixBooks
The AudioPro Home Recording Course, Volumes I, II, and III
The Art of Mixing: A Visual Guide to Recording, Engineering, and Production
The Mixing Engineer's Handbook
The Mastering Engineer's Handbook
Music Publishing: The Real Road to Music Business Success, Rev. and Exp. 5th Ed.
How to Run a Recording Session
The Professional Musician's Internet Guide
The Songwriters Guide to Collaboration, Rev. and Exp. 2nd Ed.
Critical Listening and Auditory Perception
Modular Digital Multitracks: The Power User's Guide, Rev. Ed.
Professional Microphone Techniques
Sound for Picture, 2nd Ed.
Music Producers, 2nd Ed.
Live Sound Reinforcement
Professional Sound Reinforcement Techniques
Creative Music Production: Joe Meek's Bold Techniques

Printed in Auburn Hills, MI
ISBN 1-931140-36-7

Contents

Mixing and Recording Vocals

It's amazing how sensitive, both mentally and physically, the vocalist is. Singing is an interesting blend of technical ability, physical talent, and emotional interpretation. There must be a good balance between these factors. Awareness and understanding of these factors will help you bring out the best in the singers you produce and record.

Vocals are the focal point of almost every commercial song. If the vocals sound good, the song will probably sound good. If they sound bad, the song will probably sound bad. The vocal tracks typically contain the most apparent emotional content and impact of the song. Most listeners focus on the vocals first (consciously at least).

The vocal tracks must capture the appropriate emotional and musical feel for the song. It's important that they're understandable, in tune, and that the lyrics are sung in a way that gives the song meaning. Conveying the meaning of the lyrics usually takes precedence over other factors. Small flaws in technical presentation can be justified by an authentic, emotional, heartfelt performance.

Let's start by looking at some techniques that'll help you record a good sound. Practice these techniques until they're practically instinctive and commit this information to memory. Concentrate on recording excellent vocal takes rather than simply excellent vocal sounds. An excellent take includes style, emotion, inspiration, and a good sound. A good sound by itself doesn't do much to make a song appeal to anyone.

Mic Techniques

Placement

Placement of the microphone in relation to the singer is a key variable. Not only does it matter where the mic is, but the best placement changes depending on the type of mic you're using, the room you're in, the vocal timbre, musical style, and personal taste.

Condenser microphones are usually the first choice for studio vocal applications. Commercial vocal sounds vary, but most professionally recorded hit vocals are recorded with a good condenser mic set on cardioid pickup pattern, from a distance of 6 to 12 inches. A solo or group vocal recorded at this distance sounds full and warm on most condenser mics.

If you're using a moving-coil mic, vocals sound thin and tinny from distances greater than 6 to 8 inches. If you only have a moving-coil mic, you'll get the best results when close-miking solo vocals.

Reflections

With any instrument, including vocals the sound of the instrument or voice reflecting off the walls and other hard surfaces can be either very beneficial or very harmful to the recorded sound.

Side Wall Reflections

The vocal sound reflects off each surface in the room. The side walls often play an important role in the combination between direct and reflected sound. Not only does the sound combine at the mic in a varying phase relationship as it reflects off the walls, but reflections off any hard surface in the room influence the recorded vocal sound.

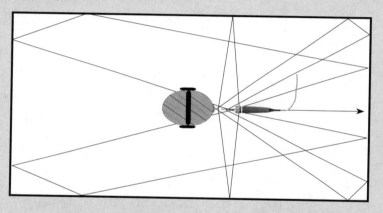

Combinations of Reflections

Each reflection combines with the original sound wave, resulting in a completely new sound wave. The summing and canceling process that occurs when sound waves combine becomes very complex when all the possible reflections are considered.

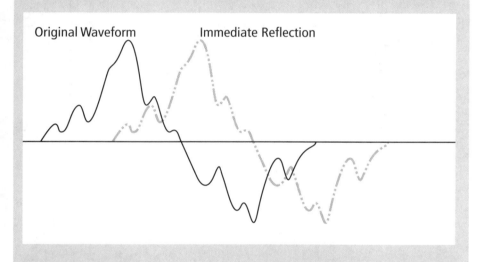

Original Waveform   Immediate Reflection

The Single Reflection

The sound of the direct voice and the single reflection combine to create a different vocal texture. Moving closer to, or farther from, a hard surface like a wall can affect the sound quality dramatically.

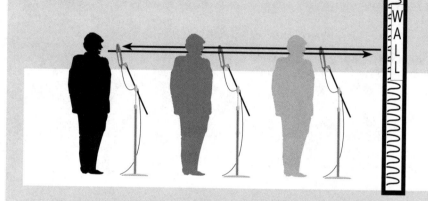

Small Room vs. Large Room

If the reflections change the sound quality at the microphone, then we should also realize that, since the size and shape of the room determine the reflections, a singer's sound changes when recorded in different rooms. Listen to Audio Examples 1–3. Each example demonstrates the effect of different rooms on my vocal sound. On each example, I'm holding the microphone about one foot from my mouth. Aside from the sound change, listen to the difference in natural room ambience.

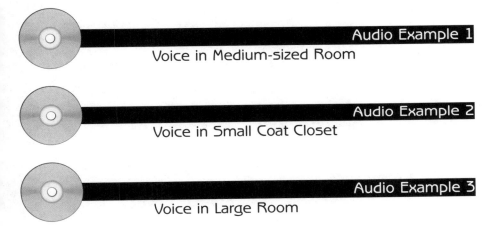

Audio Example 1
Voice in Medium-sized Room

Audio Example 2
Voice in Small Coat Closet

Audio Example 3
Voice in Large Room

Based on the previous audio examples, it's clear that the room and mic distance play an important part in the sound of the vocal. We need a good set of rules about recording vocals to help provide a starting point for our choice of recording technique. Don't feel bound by these rules—many great vocal sounds have been recorded through techniques that break the rules—but use them as a foundation for your choices. Let's consider mics in two categories:

1. Moving-coil and ribbon
2. Condenser

Moving-coil/Ribbon

Moving-coil and ribbon mics are almost always designed for close-miking applications and don't typically provide a full sound when the singer is more than six to eight inches from the mic. To get a full, natural sound from these mics, it's best to record the singer from a distance of two to six inches.

Condenser

When recording vocals in a recording studio, condenser microphones are almost always the best choice. The condenser mic operating principle is best suited to accurately capture a singer's natural sound because they color the sound less than other mic types. They also respond more accurately to transients, therefore producing a vocal sound that's very natural and understandable.

Unlike moving-coil and ribbon mics, condenser microphones sound full from a distance of one or two feet. The singer can stand back from the mic a bit and you can still record a full, present sound while retaining the option to include more or less of the room's acoustic character. Miking vocals from one or two feet away often produces a unique and transparent sound.

Acoustic Considerations

Usually in commercial popular music it's best to record vocals in a room that's acoustically neutral (doesn't have a long reverberation time) and mike the vocalist from a distance of 6 to 12 inches. This approach provides the most flexibility during mixdown. You maintain the freedom to use reverberation and other effects to artificially place the vocal in the space that best suits the emotion of the music.

Be willing to experiment with different acoustic settings. However, take care that you don't include so much room sound that the vocal loses the close intimacy that sounds good on a lot of popular music.

Positioning the Microphone

Some singers have a good, smooth sound; other singers have a nasal quality when they sing. And others tend to have a thin, edgy sound. Where you place the mic in relation to the singer will affect the tonal quality of the vocal sound. If you place the mic directly in front of the singer's mouth (pointing directly at the singer) you'll get a pretty even and natural tonal balance. But if he or she makes much noise while singing, it will come through—loud and clear—on your recorder. These noises typically include lip smacks, nose sniffs, breaths, and sometimes even the sound of air leaking through the nose while the performance is happening.

If the sound isn't good directly in front of the singer, try moving the mic up about

3 or 4 inches above the singer's mouth and pointing it down at the mouth. This usually eliminates a lot of the lip smacks and other noises, plus it cleans up the nasal sound that some singers have a problem with.

Aiming the Mic Directly at the Singer's Mouth

Both these microphones are pointing directly at the singer. The large diaphragm mics, like the one on the left, pick up from the side rather than the top. This technique might work well on a vocalist, but often the mic receives too much air, causing problems with plosives.

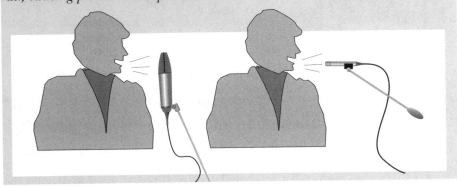

If you position the mic 4 to 6 inches below the vocalist's mouth and then aim the mic up at the mouth, you might fill out a thin sounding voice, but you might get more extraneous noises than you care to deal with.

Pointing the microphone down at the singer's mouth produces a sound with minimal nasal quality while de-emphasizing lip smacks, breaths, sniffs, etc.

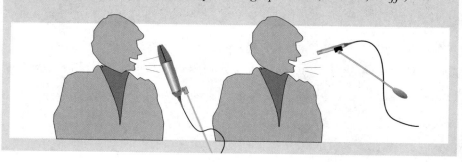

The basic microphone position is a crucial factor. Sometimes a difference of one inch in either direction will dramatically affect the quality and impact of the vocal sound. Each singer offers a different set of variables so there are no absolute solutions. Keep up the quest for the best possible sound—you'll know when you've hit the right combination.

Pointing the mic up at the singer's mouth might fill out an otherwise thin sound. However, this technique accentuates nasal tone quality as well as breaths, lip smacks and sniffs.

Windscreen

A windscreen is used in the studio to keep abundant air, caused by hard enunciation, from creating loud pops as the microphone capsule is overworked. In an outdoor application, the windscreen is also used to shield the capsule from wind.

Most vocal recordings require the use of a windscreen, also called a pop filter. When a singer pronounces words containing hard consonants, like "p" and "t," there's a lot of air hitting the mic capsule at once. When the air from these hard consonants, called plosives, hits the mic capsule, it can actually bottom out the capsule diaphragm. In other words, this "pop" can be the physical sound of the microphone diaphragm actually hitting the end of its normal travel range. On our recorder, we hear this as a loud and obvious pop. Audio Example 4 demonstrates the sound of a problem plosive. This pop is usually difficult to get rid of in the mix so it's best to find a way not to record it.

Audio Example 4
The Problem Plosive

A windscreen can diffuse the air from the singer before it gets to the mic capsule, therefore eliminating the problem plosive. Windscreens come in many different forms. Moving-coil and ribbon mics often have the windscreen built in. Most condenser mics don't have the windscreen built in. Since the condenser microphones sound

full from a distance, we can have the
singer stand back far enough that plosives
aren't much of a problem, and we'll still
get a full, natural sound. Depending on
the singer and the sound you want, you
might not be able to keep the mic far
enough away to avoid plosives while still
achieving the sound you want.

The Windscreen

*There are many different types and shapes of foam windscreens. They work
very well when used in the proper context but can adversely affect sound
quality. When placed over a mic
capsule, the sound arriving at
the capsule through the foam
windscreen is affected by the type
of foam material rather than
physical shape.*

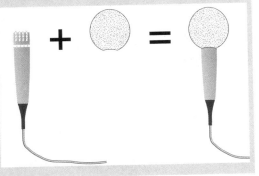

If a singer has hard enunciation, if
you're trying to get a close sound, or if
you're outside on a breezy day, try a foam
windscreen. They're available in different

shapes, sizes and colors, but they're all made from molded porous foam. Their purpose is to diffuse the air before it reaches the mic capsule. Foam windscreens are the typical choice for outdoor applications because they surround the mic capsule completely and offer the most complete

Embroidery Hoop Windscreen

This windscreen uses a piece of a nylon stocking stretched over an embroidery hoop and attached to the bottom part of a standard mic clip. Most embroidery hoops fit very nicely in the mic clip that comes with a Shure SM57 or SM58. This design alters the vocal sound less than most other windscreen designs.

An added bonus to this screen is its flexibility in positioning. If the sound you need requires the vocalist to stand one foot (or any other specified distance) from the microphone, simply position the windscreen on a mic stand one foot from the mic capsule. The singer is then given a visual reference to gauge distance from the mic and a barrier to keep from moving too close.

wind diffusion. Purists often reject foam windscreens for any use other than outdoor applications because they muffle the sound and attenuate the high frequencies more than the other designs.

Another type of windscreen can be constructed from a piece of an old panty hose, an embroidery hoop and a mic clip. This design works very well, is inexpensive and typically sounds much better than foam.

Attaching the Windscreen to the Mic Stand

The embroidery hoop screen can be attached to a regular mic stand with a special clamp—normally used in live applications to hold a guitar mic on the same mic stand as the singer/guitarist's vocal mic.

Mounting the hoop on a long goose neck lets you easily position the screen while eliminating the need for a separate mic stand.

Using a Pencil For a Windscreen

Here's another type of windscreen that's inexpensive, convenient, and quite effective. Tape a pencil to the microphone so that it lies directly in front of the mic diaphragm—deflecting air that heads straight at it—therefore eliminating unwanted pops. This technique has little effect on vocal sound quality.

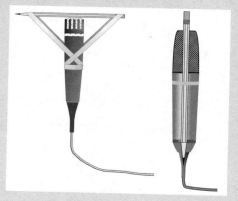

The nylon, stretched over the hoop and placed between the singer's mouth and the microphone, usually diffuses the air enough to avoid plosives and muffles than the sound less than a foam windscreen. This tool is also commercially available.

Try taping a pencil to the mic so it goes across the front of the mic capsule. If the pencil is directly in front of the center of the mic capsule, it will diffuse the air enough to eliminate the pops. This technique works best on large capsule mics.

Listen to Audio Examples 5–8. These four different examples use the same vocalist through the same setup. The only thing that changes is the windscreen.

Audio Example 5

No Windscreen

Audio Example 6 demonstrates the use of a foam windscreen over the mic. Listen for a difference in the high-frequency content.

Audio Example 6

Foam Windscreen

Audio Example 7 was recorded using an embroidery hoop with nylon stretched over it. This windscreen has a different and subtle effect on the vocal sound.

Nylon over an Embroidery Hoop

The vocal in Audio Example 8 was recorded with a pencil taped to the mic so that it runs across the center of the mic diaphragm.

Pencil Across the Diaphragm

Avoiding Plosive Problems

Sometimes even using a good windscreen won't eliminate all pops. Try the following three techniques along with, or instead of, a windscreen.

1. Move the mic slightly above or below the singer's mouth. This'll get the air moving past the diaphragm instead of moving directly at it. There might be a slight sound difference, which could be

either detrimental or beneficial, but this is typically a good way to avoid pops.

2. Point the mic at an angle to the vocalist. This position, like the previous suggestion, allows the air to move past the capsule instead of at it.

3. Move the mic very close to the vocalist (closer than two inches). The movement of air doesn't reach its peak energy until it's gone more than an inch or so from the singer's mouth so you might be able to position the mic at a point before the air achieves maximum flow, therefore avoiding pops. Positioning the vocalist close to the microphone works best on moving-coil microphones. Condenser mics suffer from close proximity to the singer because the moisture from the vocalist has an adverse effect on the sound and operational status of the mic.

The Proximity Effect

If you're using a condenser mic to record a vocal sound that's very close and inti-mate-sounding, you might choose to close-mike the vocalist. You'll need to use a condenser mic that has a bass roll-off switch. The bass roll-off is built into most condenser mics and typically turns down the frequencies below 75 or 80Hz. Any time a singer or narrator moves close to a microphone, the low frequencies get louder in relation to the high frequencies. This can result in a boomy or thick sound, especially if the voice is being recorded through a high quality condenser mic. Low frequencies increasing as the mic distance decreases is called the proximity effect. This effect is the most extreme when using a cardioid pickup pattern.

Bass Roll-off

Rolling off the lows lets you get a close sound without getting a thick, boomy sound. Some condenser microphones have a variable bass roll-off that will turn the lows down below a couple different user-selectable frequencies.

Bass Roll-off

Most condenser microphones offer a bass roll-off feature. A switch somewhere on the mic body lets you apply the roll-off. Some mic designs even give you a choice between roll-off frequencies and contain a small switch near the bass of the mic housing that is user adjustable. You choose between flat (often labeled LINEAR, LIN, Flat) and specific roll-off frequencies (possibly 60, 75, 80, 150 or 175).

A bass roll-off doesn't simply cut a band centered on a specific frequency. Instead, it turns everything below a specific frequency down at a rate indicated in dB per octave.

An 80Hz bass roll-off might cut the frequencies below 80Hz at a rate of 12dB per octave. In this case, at 40Hz (one octave below 80Hz) a 12dB decrease in amplitude is realized. At 20Hz (two octaves below 80Hz) a 24dB decrease in amplitude is realized.

Listen to Audio Examples 9, 10 and 11. Notice how the vocal sound changes with the adjustment of the bass roll-off.

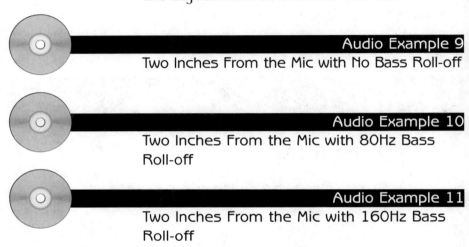

Audio Example 9
Two Inches From the Mic with No Bass Roll-off

Audio Example 10
Two Inches From the Mic with 80Hz Bass Roll-off

Audio Example 11
Two Inches From the Mic with 160Hz Bass Roll-off

Pickup Patterns

Some condenser mics have selectable pickup patterns. In other words, one mic can be switched to cardioid, omni, bidirectional and sometimes hypercardioid. These are called the microphone's directional characteristics.

Sound Advice on Recording and Mixing Vocals

Roll-off at 160Hz

The graph below represents the frequency response of a microphone set to roll-off the lows below 160Hz. A bass roll-off is also called a high pass filter because it lets the frequencies above a specific point pass through unaffected.

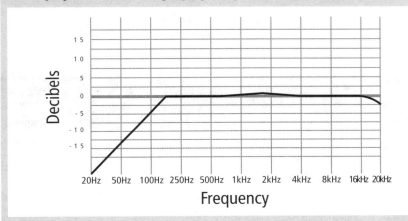

Each pickup pattern offers a different sound, and each of these sounds might be useful in different ways. Experiment with variations between pickup patterns and mic distance. Once you find the combination of mic choice, pattern selection and mic distance that adds life, emotion and superior natural sound quality to a vocal part, you won't turn back. If you spend a little extra time perfecting your mic technique, you'll gain it back several times over as your music comes together with greater ease, inspiration, and confidence. Good mic technique adds depth to a vocal track that you simply can't get with equalization and other processing.

Cardioid Pattern

A cardioid microphone hears best from the front and actively rejects sounds from behind, producing a heart-shaped pickup pattern. When using a cardioid mic, you can point the mic at the sound you want to record and away from the sound you don't want to record. Rejection of sound from behind the microphone isn't complete, but it's sufficient enough to help minimize unwanted sounds.

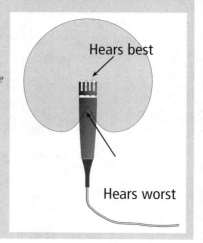

Hears best

Hears worst

Omnidirectional Pattern

A microphone with an omnidirectional pickup pattern hears equally from all directions—it doesn't reject sound from any direction. Most omnidirectional mics use a condenser capsule. Since they don't reject sounds from any direction, omni mics are an excellent choice for capturing room ambience.

360° spherical pickup pattern

Omnidirectional microphones are least susceptible to timbre changes created by variations in the distance of the mic from the sound source.

Bidirectional Pattern

Bidirectional microphones hear equally well from both sides, but they don't pick up sound from the edges (90° off-axis). This directional characteristic is also called the figure-eight pattern.

Bidirectional mics work very well when recording two voices or instruments to one track because they induce minimal phase cancelation.

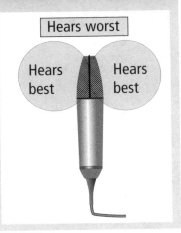

Hears worst

Hears best   Hears best

Hypercardioid Pattern

The hypercardioid directional characteristic is narrower than the traditional cardioid pattern—it doesn't hear as well from the sides as the cardioid mic. In addition, there's an area of sensitivity directly behind the mic (180° off axis) that isn't present in the cardioid mic.

Hypercardioid mics work well when the sound sources are close together but you want minimal interaction between the microphones.

Supercardioid Pattern

The terms supercardioid and hypercardioid are often used interchangeably. In reality, the supercardioid pattern is wider than the hypercardioid pattern—it hears better from the sides.

Hypercardioid and supercardioid mics both work well when you'd like to include room ambience in a controlled amount. They provide less ambience than an omnidirectional mic, but more than a cardioid mic.

Compression

Compressor/Limiter

Vocalists almost always use a wide dynamic range during the course of a song. Often they'll sing very tenderly and quietly during one measure and then emotionally blast you with all the volume and energy they can muster up during the next. Most of the time you need a compressor/limiter to avoid overloading your recorder with signal.

As the compressor's VCA (voltage controlled amplifier) turns down the signal that passes the threshold, the entire vocal track occupies a narrower dynamic range. When the vocal is in a narrow dynamic range, the loud sounds are easier to record because they aren't out of control, plus the softer sounds can be heard and understood better in the mix.

Even though the most common vocal recording technique utilizes a compressor/limiter, your choice to include a compressor in your vocal recordings should be based on the vocalist, the song, vocal range, dynamic range, emotion, and other musical considerations. Avoid ruts. Evaluate each situation separately.

Vocals are usually compressed using a medium-fast attack time (3–5ms), a medium-long release time (from a half second to a second), and a ratio between 3:1 and 7:1 with about 6dB of gain reduction at the loudest part of the track.

A vocalist who is used to recording in the studio can make your job much easier. Less compression is needed on singers who use mic technique to compensate for their changes in level. A seasoned professional will back off a bit on the loud notes and move in a bit on the soft notes. This technique on the vocalist's part will help you record the most controlled, understandable and natural sounding vocal track. If you set the compressor so it indicates no gain reduction most of the time with 2 to

4dB of reduction on the loudest notes, and if the vocal is always understandable and smooth sounding, that's good.

Listen to the vocal track with rhythm accompaniment in Audio Example 12. The vocal isn't compressed. Notice how it sometimes disappears in the mix.

Audio Example 13 demonstrates the same vocal, compressed using a ratio of 4:1 with up to about 6dB of gain reduction. This time the peak level is the same but listen for the softer notes. They're easier to hear and understand.

Sibilance

Avoid overcompressing the vocals. If the attack time isn't instantaneous or at least nearly instantaneous, it's possible to compress most of the words but not the initial sounds. For instance, a word starting with "s" or "t" might have a very fast attack—an attack too fast to be turned down by the compressor. The initial "s" or "t" will sound unnaturally loud and, like other transient sounds, won't register accurately on a VU meter. These exaggerated attacks are called sibilant sounds. When sibilant sounds are recorded too hot, your recordings will have a splatting type of distortion every time sibilance occurs. Sibilance distortion also happens when a sibilant sound occurs in the middle or at the end of a word.

Each singer has a unique sibilant character. Bone structure, physical alignment of the vocalist's teeth, jaw position and size all play a part in exactly how singers produce sibilant sounds. Some vocalists don't produce strong transients; other vocalists produce megatransients. I find that a singer with straight teeth and a perfect bite typically produces a very strong transient on

Sound Advice on Recording and Mixing Vocals

consonants that have a "hiss" sound ("s,"
"t," "ch," "zh," "sh").

Sibilance

These graphs represent the changes in amplitude over time of the word "Sally."
The top graph has an average level of about 0VU, but the "S" is about 3dB
above the remainder of the word "...ally."

If the compressor's attack time is slow enough that the VCA doesn't begin to act
until after the "S" and if the remainder
of the word is compressed, exaggeration
of the initial sibilant sound results.

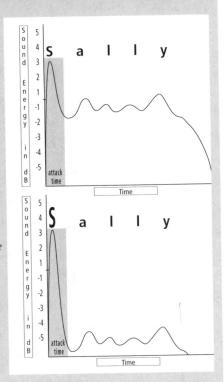

The bottom graph represents the result of
compressing the word "Sally." Notice the
difference in level between the "S" and
the remainder of the word. This type of
compression technique, when used in
moderation (1 to 3dB), can help increase
intelligibility and understandability.
However, this scenario leads to overexag-
gerated sibilance that degrades your
music, especially in cassette duplication.

Sibilance problems often slide by when recording to the multitrack (analog or digital), but when cassettes are duplicated you might find a big problem with sibilance distortion. Small tape has less headroom and therefore distorts easier than most multitrack recorders.

The De-esser

Use a de-esser to compensate for sibilance problems. A de-esser is a fast acting compressor set to turn down the high frequencies that are present in the sibilant sounds, and it is often built into a compressor/limiter. If the de-esser is activated, the VCA responds to the highs instead of all frequencies at once, therefore turning down the exaggerated sibilance. De-essers often have a control that sweeps a range of high frequencies, letting the user choose which high frequency will be compressed. The threshold control lets you set the de-esser so it only turns down the high frequencies of the sibilant sounds but leaves the rest of the track alone.

Sound Advice on Recording and Mixing Vocals

Good compression technique, proper mic choice and positioning are usually the answer to sibilance problems. But these problems have become particularly problematic with the growth of digital recording. Digital metering helps you record the full range of the transient accurately so any transfer to analog mediums, such as cassette tape, provide opportunity for sibilance distortion. Through education and the proper use of compression and de-essing, you can record vocal tracks that are clean and clear and work well within any musical structure.

Listen to the vocal in Audio Example 14 as it's overcompressed, exaggerating the sibilance. The compressor in this example is set to a medium-slow attack time, letting the sibilance pass through uncompressed. The ratio is at 7:1 with up to 15dB of gain reduction.

Audio Example 14

Exaggerated Sibilance

Equalization

When tracking vocals to the multitrack, apply equalization only if necessary after positioning the best sounding microphone for the best possible sound. If you print an extremely equalized vocal to the multitrack, you're making EQ decisions that are best reserved for mixdown. Once the final instrumentation and orchestration choices are made, you can make intelligent decisions based on the final textural support. It's better to work with a good raw sound during mixdown than to fight an EQ problem you created in over-aggressive tracking. During mixdown it's often necessary to EQ the vocals to help them stand out in the mix. Frequencies that need to be cut or boosted are dependent on the orchestration of the completed arrangement.

If you're using very few tracks or doing a live stereo recording of an entire group, it might be necessary to boost the presence range on the voice (between 3 and 5kHz) to increase the understandability of the part. Also, try cutting the lows (below about 80Hz) to give the voice a more transparent, clear sound.

Recording Environment

The voice is the most personal of instruments. Most of the magic in a vocal performance comes from the emotional interpretation of the true meaning in a song. We might have all our ducks neatly in a row technically, but if the singer isn't feeling comfortable, secure and confident, there's a good chance that the vocal recording won't be all that spectacular.

The producer and engineer set the emotional tone for the session. If they're uptight and impatient, guess how the session will go? "Not well" would be a good guess. If the producer and engineer are positive and emotionally supportive, they can usually get an artist to perform beyond everyone's expectations.

Only the most experienced and self confident singers can walk into an emotionally dead, cluttered, poorly lit, uncomfortably cold and clammy room and instantly start performing tender and meaningful lyrics with believability.

It's your job as the engineer or producer to see to it that the vocal room is at a comfortable temperature, that the lighting is soft and flattering, and that there isn't a lot of clutter around. Create a mood in the room. Singing is an emotional art. Get the singer into the right emotional frame of mind.

Intonation

Sometimes during a take it's obvious to everyone that the singer is consistently out of tune. This even happens with singers that always seem to have great intonation.

So why do they, all of a sudden, start singing sharp or flat when it comes down to recording?

Many young singers simply haven't learned enough about their craft to endure the tedium and scrutiny of the recording world. Even though that fact is brutal, you as the engineer/producer are commissioned with the awesome duty of making the best of the situations you're given.

Often a singer is out of tune simply because the headphone mix is providing an inaccurate pitch reference or a pitch reference that's hard to pinpoint. Always listen to the headphone mix when you're getting the singer set up. It's even a good idea for you to plug headphones into the same mix they're getting so that you'll know instantly when something's not right.

For pitch reference, the best instruments to include in the headphone mix are piano and clean guitar. Some of the big keyboard sounds include chorus, re-verbs and other effects which tend to obscure the pitch center. A clean, non-effected piano or guitar definitively identifies the tonal center.

Singers often sing with better intonation when they uncover one of their ears rather than letting the headphones cover both ears. Simply moving one side of the headphones behind the ear lets singers hear themselves more like they would in a live setting. This simple technique has the potential to fix intonation problems instantly!

When the headphones are too loud or when they have fluid-filled ear pieces (tightly enclosing the ear), most singers sing flat. Open, foam headphones are good for intonation but bad for head-phone leakage.

Singers usually like to hear a little reverb or echo in the phones while they're singing. A little reverb is usually okay when tracking, but less reverb in the phones generally results in more accurate vocal tracks.

Punch In Punch Out

The voice is fairly fragile, and many singers wear out pretty quickly in comparison to instrumentalists. To continually re-record complete takes in order to get the perfect pass isn't practical. Be sure the singers you record understand that punching in is common and that even the best of singers use this advantage of multitrack recording. Sometimes inexperienced singers expect to walk into a session, sing the part once, have everyone ooh and ah and start collecting the royalties. But singing in a session is hard work and demands a lot of time to perfect each performance. I'm sure you'd like to feel good about your recordings for the next 30 or 40 years so spend the time to get it right.

Good engineers develop the knack for timing the punch-in. A good punch combined with a good performance will be so smooth that no one would ever guess the insert wasn't recorded at the same time as the rest of the track. Concentrate and focus on the punch-in. As the engineer (and/or producer), you hold the authority to ask all nonessential personnel to leave the studio while you and others essential to the task at hand complete the job with great excellence. It's easy to be distracted when other people are hanging around, and staying focused is necessary. Nobody has ever expressed anything but appreciation when I've politely asked people to leave for the good of the recording project.

Panning

Lead vocals are traditionally panned to the center position. This keeps them the center focal point and, since they're usually very strong in the mix, distributes the vocal energy evenly between the left and right channels. Sometimes certain vocal effects are panned evenly to left and right for a big sound, but no matter what effects we use, the entire lead vocal sound should be evenly balanced between left and right.

Background vocals can be panned left and right depending on how many tracks there are, but the entire backing track should still be spread out evenly between left and right.

Common Vocal Effects

In recording, it's our goal to produce a sound that's natural, but we need to keep in perspective which acoustical environment we're trying to make it sound natural in. There isn't much that's natural about the sound of a vocalist in a deadened studio singing into one microphone. As engineers, we take that raw sound and through the use of reverb and other effects, place it in the environment that would make it fun to listen to. Effects simulate the proper acoustical ambience for specific musical styles.

Slapback Delay

A slapback is a single repeat of the original signal. The delay time on this single repeat must be longer than 35ms to be categorized as a slapback, with the most common slap-back delay times between 120 and 300ms. Delays blur variations in intonation and generally give the vocal a rich and interesting sound.

The initial delay of the direct sound is what gives the brain its perception of the size of the room the sound is in. The longer the slapback, the larger the room. A slapback can make a vocal sound very big fast, before the addition of reverb. The single delay has a cleaner sound than lots of reverb. Often lead vocals have no reverb, just delay. Listen to the dry vocal track in Audio Example 15.

The Dry Vocal

Audio Example 16 demonstrates the same part with a slapback delay panned center. Notice how much more interesting this simple effect makes the lead vocal.

Audio Example 16
The Single Slapback

The delay in Audio Example 16 is in time with the eighth note of this song. Most delays work best if they relate in some way to the tempo of the song.

Another common delay effect involves the use of a short slapback as a thickener. This technique utilizes a delay time between about 35 and 75ms. This procedure involves the main lead vocal panned to the center position supported by a thickening delay (also panned center). Bring the level of the delay up, behind the main vocal until the combination sounds fuller and larger than just the original—but not so far that the vocal sounds unnatural.

The Electronic Double

Doubling combines the vocal with a delay that's less than 35ms. This effect works very well on backing vocals and sometimes on lead vocals. Typically, the original is panned to one side with the delay panned to the other. This gives a wide stereo effect and can provide a great sound in stereo. Caution! Always check these doubling effects in mono. As we've discovered in previous chapters, combining short delays to a mono mix can result in total or partial cancellation of the track. This is never a good thing to do to your lead vocal track. Listen to the mix in mono and adjust the delay time until the sound is full and natural sounding. This'll assure you that the track will sound good in mono and stereo.

In Audio Example 17, you'll hear the dry vocal panned center. Then I'll turn up

the 19ms delayed vocal on the right as I
pan the dry vocal left.

Audio Example 17

The Electronic Double

A double produces a very big sound
that's fun to listen to as long as you've
cross-checked to mono. In Audio Example
18, I'll sum the stereo mix to mono and
adjust the delay time in 1ms increments.
Notice the extreme differences on some of
the changes.

Audio Example 18

Delay Changes in Mono

Regeneration

If you've used a slapback but want a little
fuller sound, try regenerating the delay.
This makes the delay repeat more times.
When I'm regenerating I'll usually set the
delay up to repeat four or five times and
typically set the delay time between 200
and 300ms.

Reverb

The most common effect on vocals is reverberation. Even a marginal vocal track can sound pretty good all by itself if you pour enough reverb on it. Excessive reverberation can put a haze over the sound of your mix and give your music an amateur sound. Most current reverberation devices let you control reverb times, predelays, pre-echoes, EQ and most any parameter you could imagine controlling. This flexibility actually puts more responsibility on the engineer to achieve a specific sound that fits a song.

Ballads in most styles sound good with long reverb times, between two and four seconds on the lead vocal. The decaying reverberation blends the space that exists between the beats of a slow tempo ballad. Hall and chamber reverb sounds fill a song the best, in most cases, because of their dark, rich sound. The ballad in Audio Example 19 uses hall reverb with a delay time of 2.6 seconds and a predelay of 60ms.

Audio Example 19

Hall Reverb on a Ballad

The sound of hall and chamber reverberation tends to get covered up on faster songs that contain a lot of different rhythmic and harmonic parts. There has to be so much reverb to actually hear the effect that the mix sounds very muddy. Bright reverb works better on fast songs; plates, some room sounds and bright chamber sounds work best.

Predelay

The predelay setting can simulate the sound of slapback delay with reverberation occurring only after the slapback. This feature is very useful. Predelay replaces the simple slapback echo with the delayed, 100 percent wet reverberation. We keep the clean effect of the slapback while adding the filling effect of reverb. Every vocal note is heard clean and dry for the first instant, only to be followed and filled out by smooth reverberation. Using short decay times (between .5 and 1 second) and long predelays (between 100 and 250ms) produces vocal sounds that are very big and impressive while maintaining a tight sounding mix. The vocal in Audio Example 20 has a predelay of 120ms and a decay time of .7 seconds.

Audio Example 20
120ms Predelay with .7 Second Decay

Backing Vocals

First of all, use as few mics as possible to get the job done. If you have four singers in one room, the temptation is to set up four separate mics to get a good controlled blend at the mixer. With this type of setup there's typically so much phase interaction between the four mics that the overall sound of the vocals takes a nose dive, and won't sound full and

Sound Advice on Recording and Mixing Vocals

clean, especially when you're recording in a small room.

Try using one good microphone, in omni or bidirectional setting. Move the singers around the mic until you find the blend you need. Once you get a good performance recorded, try recording it again on another track. This live doubling technique produces very big, full-sounding backing vocals. Have the singers change places on the doubled take to capture a little different blend, adding to the dimension of the live double.

If you want ultimate control of the vocal blend during mixdown, record the singers at the same time but isolate each singer in separate rooms, using separate mics. Or, record them one at a time to different tracks. This technique eats up tracks fast but allows you flexibility in the mixdown, plus it gives you the ability to get each part just right, one at a time, instead of trying to get the entire group to sing it right or simultaneously.

Mixing Techniques

A lot of mixing might be required on the lead vocal track. The primary focal point of the mix is almost always the lead vocal. Because of this, it has to maintain a constant space in the mix. The style of the music generally determines exactly how loud the lead vocal should be in relation to the rest of the band; once that's been determined, the relationship must remain constant.

- Build a list of moves for the duration of your song, referenced to the recorder counter or time code.
- A lyric sheet is very useful. Mark your moves, with the tape counter number, by the lyric. It's usually easier to follow the lyrics than just numbers, but often a simple list of counter numbers, in the

order that they occur with specific notes, is the ideal approach.

- If a fader or any other control is constantly moving from one position to another, mark the two or three positions on the board with a grease pencil. These marks are easily removed and provide instant visual cues.

Mix Moves - The List Approach

Counter Number	Channel Number	Control Position	Notes
0021	5	-5	Intro Keyboards
0036	5	-9	
0036	3	ON and -1	
0048	3	+1	Fader moves on "tears"
0102	3	OFF	
0109	7	+2.5	Guitar Solo
0210	7	OFF	End of Guitar Solo
0211	3	ON	
0222	5	+1	Keyboard Fill
0224	5	-5	
0312	1 and 2	ON and -2	Backing Vocals Enter

Use up and down arrows to indicate instrumental or vocal level changes; circle the change points.

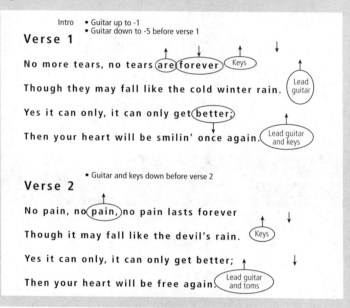

In a heavy R&B or rock song, the lead vocal is often buried into the mix a little. The result of this kind of balance is rhythmic drive and punchy drums; the bass and primary harmony instruments are accentuated.

In Audio Example 21, I've mixed the vocal back a bit. When the volume is turned up on this kind of mix, the rhythm section is very strong and punchy.

Audio Example 21
The Vocal Back Mix

In Audio Example 22, I boost the vocals in the mix. When the vocals are forward in the mix, it becomes very important to avoid vocal passages that are very loud in relation to the rest of the track. Notice how the vocal becomes difficult to listen to as it gets too loud on this passage.

Audio Example 22
The Vocals Louder

In a country or commercial pop song, the lead vocal is usually loud in the mix, allowing the lyric and emotion of the vocal performance to be easily heard and felt by the listener.

When the lead vocal is being mixed, there are many times when one word or syllable will need to be turned up or down; sometimes the changes are more general. This the point where you, as the mixer, need to have a copy of the lyrics. The more organized you can be, the quicker your mix will go.

Chances are you'll have several changes to make during the mix, and the lead vocal will probably contain many of them. Mark the recorder counter numbers on the lyric sheet at each verse, chorus, interlude, and bridge; this will help speed things up, no matter what. As you develop a list of vocal level changes, write them on the lyric sheet next to, above, or below the lyric closest to the move. Lead sheets are very convenient for keeping track of mix moves.

Working Digitally

Most digital editing and recording packages display audio data in a graphic waveform. This waveform shows exactly what the sound is doing. If it gets louder, the waveform gets bigger; if there's silence, the waveform display is a straight line. Editing becomes nearly as visual as it is aural.

In the waveform view, it's easy to trim off either end to eliminate unwanted data, or even to remove data from anywhere within the waveform. If the recording went on for a few seconds too long, it's very easy to slide the end of the waveform to the left, trimming the excess. Only the portion of the wave that's seen is heard.

Punch-in

The punch-in, when using a hard disk recorder, holds a different level of intensity and precision than when using a tape-based recorder. In the tape-based domain, the punch-in is destructive—one mistake and an entire phrase might be ruined.

Visual Assistance from Waveform Editing

In the waveform below the announcer says, "...and the guitar player is about to play his best lick, uh, ever." He emphasizes the "uh" and it sounds unprofessional. With waveform editing, problems like this are very easy to spot and repair. Simply locate the problem word or sound, highlight it, and remove it.

And the guitar player was about to play his best lick,   uhhhhhhhhhhhhh,   ever.

And the guitar player was about to play his best   lick,   ever.

Audio 1-02-03

There is an art to tape-based punch-ins. The operator learns to punch in and out of record with amazing precision.

Sound Advice on Recording and Mixing Vocals

Replacing a word or portion of a word is common. However, one slip of the finger, one note held a little too long by the performer, and the material before, during, and after the intended record zone is damaged, usually irreparably.

With the advent of computer-based recording, the art form of punching in and out of record is dying. No longer do the recordist and the artist need to work perfectly together in the same "zone" to perform the perfect series of punches repeatedly. Most computer-based systems offer a "fast punch" option, but if you happen to make a mistake, it's no big deal. Simply access the waveform edit window and resize the audio boxes to include whatever you need from the old and new takes. Even if it sounds like you cut off part of the original audio, it can be easily resurrected and positioned to perfection. No problem!

Fixing the Digital Punch-in

Even though the punch-in, circled on B, looks like it erases over some of the good part of the take, all is well because the data still exists. Simply grab the end of the waveform blocks to close in or open up the waveform blocks. Once the edit point in B is moved to the right on the new lyric, the original good take can be opened back up to include the portion that appeared to be erased. Digital editing like this provides ample freedom to experiment without the fear of ruining anything. Even when it looks like damage is done, it probably isn't.

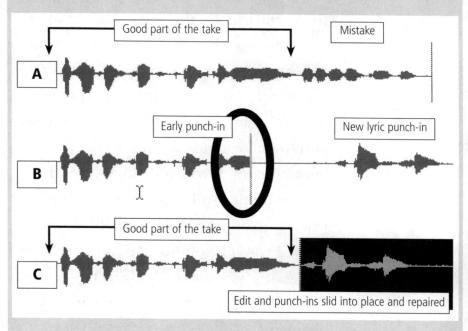

Good part of the take — Mistake

A

Early punch-in — New lyric punch-in

B

Good part of the take

C

Edit and punch-ins slid into place and repaired

Channels, Tracks, and Takes

A few terms are often used interchangeably, although they refer to different interrelated functions. Tracks, channels, and takes are not all the same. These words need to be differentiated so the concepts can be understood and put into practice.

Channels reside on a mixer. Each of the identical rows of faders, knobs, and buttons is a channel. To say a system has 24 channels refers only to the mixer, not to the multitrack recording capabilities.

Tracks are individual recording zones on a multitrack recorder. A 24-track analog tape recorder has 24 separate portions spread evenly across the width of tape. Audio is recorded separately across the horizontal distance of the tape. A modular digital multitrack operates on the same horizontal track scheme.

The computer-based digital recorder also has tracks. Although there's no tape, a track is still represented on a list and the onscreen transport operates along a horizontal line like the tape-based systems.

A track, in a digital system, typically has provisions for its own level, balance, equalization, and routing control (its own channel) within the software realm, just as it would in a traditional analog setup.

Takes add another dimension to tracks. When a track is created and the instrument is recorded, you're done—in the tape-based domain. The computer setup, on the other hand, provides for multiple takes on each track. Without creating another track, a completely separate take can be recorded. In this way, the track list remains small and manageable, while the possibilities for creating options for each track are virtually limitless—depending on available disk space.

Comping

Comping is a technique that has been used in the multitrack world for about as long as multitrack recording has been in existence. The concept is simple—find the best parts from several takes, then compile them into one track that represents the performance in the very best way.

Once you've recorded a good take, record another take, but save the old version. The computer-based system allows for plenty of takes, so let the singer fly a bit. Record several takes straight through the song. Stop as seldom as possible. Only stop to focus on a section that you know hasn't quite made it to the perfection of the previous takes. When you have several takes and you're convinced that each section has been performed to the highest standards, you've succeeded.

The actual comping process involves reevaluating each take. Use a lyric sheet to mark the best take for each lyric. Once you're convinced you know where each chunk of brilliance is located, start compiling all the sections to one new track. Simply copy from the source takes, then paste to the new comped track.

Comping the Lead Vocal

It's common to record several versions of a track for review at a later date. Comping is the art of compiling portions from various takes in a way that sounds like one excellent take. When performed with skill, this procedure is transparent—it sounds like the tracks were always meant to be the way they end up. Comping vocal tracks lets the artist keep the best of each take. It also provides a system that lifts a little pressure off singers.

TAKE 1	The prince and the poet found romance in South Hampton.
TAKE 2	The prince and the poet found romance in South Hampton.
TAKE 3	The prince and the poet found romance in South Hampton.
TAKE 4	The prince and the poet found romance in South Hampton.
TAKE 5	The prince and the poet found romance in South Hampton.
COMP	The prince and the poet found romance in South Hampton.

Once all the preferred sections are in place, some adjustments to edit points, level, equalization, or pitch might be necessary. There's usually a way to get the comped track to sound smooth and natural, as if it was the only take of the day. Crossfading between regions serves to smooth out many rough spots.

Tuning

A great sounding recording that was made prior to the technological boon we're in commands much respect. There are musical problems that we almost routinely repair and perfect today; our predecessors would have toiled for hours to achieve similar results. We take for granted the minute control available to each of us regarding intonation, timing, and all the mix parameters.

Intonation is definitely an attribute that we, as modern recordists, can effectively manipulate. If a note is a little out of tune, we don't need to ruin the singer trying to get it a little closer. We can simply tune it.

With the auto-tune software packages available now, it's not even necessary to have a good ear or perfect pitch to insure that all vocals or instruments are in tune. Simply set the parameters within the software package and process the desired audio; your part will be tuned to your specified perfection. Auto-Tune by Antares provides 19 different scales to reference intonation, along with the facility for graphical interface, vibrato (leaving it alone and creating it), and tolerance settings. Mackie offers an auto-tune plug-in for their D8B Digital Mixer that's also very impressive—and it's right in the console.

Audio Example 23
Out of Tune Vocal

Audio Example 24
Automatic Vocal Retuning

Sound Advice on Recording and Mixing Vocals

Automatic Tuning

Automatic tuning programs offer digital pitch analysis and repair. In the time it takes the player or singer to perform with inaccurate intonation, the processor can analyze the pitch, guess where the tonal center should have been, and repair the problem. This all happens in real-time or phrases can be processed individually and saved as new data. Special scale types can be indicated as well as the type and degree of vibrato included, or created.

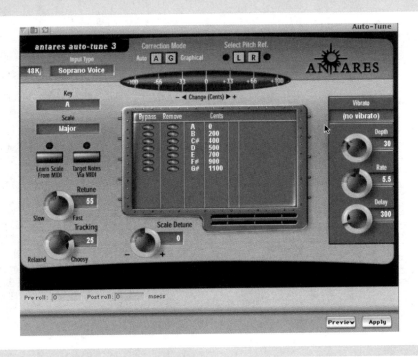

Finding the Groove

Shifting tracks in time is a feature unique to the digital era. In the analog, tape-based domain, a singer or instrumentalist is required to control the performance relative to the groove. In the digital domain, though ideally the musician will produce the very best possible performance, if a portion is a bit out of the pocket (not in time) it can be easily slid into place.

When vocals are recorded along with a MIDI sequence, finding the groove becomes extremely easy. The MIDI beat grid is typically right there onscreen. With graphic waveforms built along with the sequence, the beginnings of notes and words are simple to spot at a given location. Slide the audio waveform back and forth until the feel is right.

With controls like these available, it becomes increasingly important that the recordist have musical skills, understanding, and opinions. A technical engineer with

Sound Advice on Recording and Mixing Vocals

no basis for making musical judgement calls must rely on the expertise of a skilled and experienced musician to effectively use the features and flexibility available in today's musical tools.

Breaths

One of the worst things to do on any vocal track is to eliminate all breaths. For a track to sound, natural, real, and believable, some breaths need to be heard; they make the recording sound alive. However, they shouldn't be so loud that they're distracting to the lead vocals or to the instrumental bed.

With a digital editor, breaths during backing vocals can easily be turned down, left out, or repositioned. The most important consideration is the groove. If the breaths are left in as part of the track's life, they need to be in time with the groove. If they're not, move them, turn them down, or eliminate them. Musical judgement is the key.

Entrances

One of the primary indicators of well-sung, cleanly performed backing vocals is the precision of the entrances. If every part starts together, they'll probably stay together, often all the way through the release.

Entrances are easy to place. It's always clear where the waveform begins and, when the backing vocal tracks are lined up vertically, any part that's slightly out of time is instantly detectable. The computer-based digital recording system is laid out perfectly for fine tuning these details. The previous two illustrations demonstrate how easy it is to see when tracks are out of the groove and how simple it is to slide the segments into place to produce a precise vocal performance.

Sloppy Entrances

Notice how the backing vocals (A, B, and C) don't line up perfectly with the lead vocal. In the analog domain, this scenario is difficult and time consuming to correct. In the computer-based digital domain repairing this problem is as easy as clicking on the waveform and sliding it into perfect rhythmic alignment.

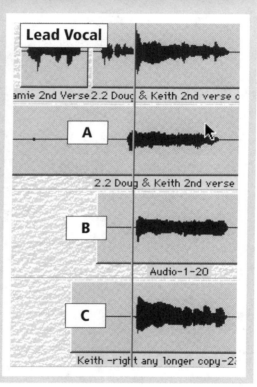

Cleaned Up Entrances

Here the entrances have been moved into position so all backing vocal tracks (A, B, and C) line up rhythmically with the lead vocal. Now all parts work together as a unit and the sound is impressive and powerful. It's always ideal to get the vocal parts as close to perfect as possible during tracking. However, if the singers are having difficulty and the session is growing long, this technique is a life saver.

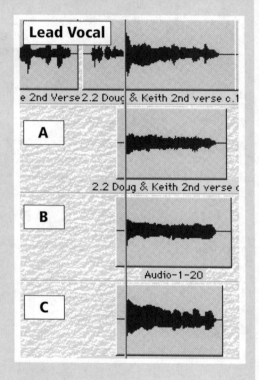

Releases

Releases are nearly as important as entrances to the polished feel of a song. The most critical releases are transient releases. Words that end in s, t, k, sh, and ch sounds are very distracting when the tracks lack precision.

With a digital editor and some patience, these ending sounds can be easily lined up with great precision after the fact. As with breath placement, these sounds should fit together nicely with the groove. Transients act like additional percussion instruments in most cases, so they should be placed with that in mind.

Readjusting Formants

Detuning fattens because it changes the overtone structure of the vocal sound, simulating the effect of a different vocalist or group on the altered track. With modern digital editing packages, formants can be adjusted separate from pitch.

Since formants control the apparent size of the voices, independent of the pitch, this adjustment can produce some amazing vocal effects. Alter the formant slightly on one of the backing vocal tracks for a fat sound.

Conclusion

Many of the techniques described in this book are commonly used in tracking and during mixdown. Always assess vocal mixing and recording tasks with musical and emotional considerations. Begin incorporating these techniques immediately. Some will fit your style and some won't, but they all add to the repertoire of recording tricks you offer to every creative endeavour.